Properties of Matter

Length and Width

Arthur Best

Cavendish
Square

New York

Published in 2019 by Cavendish Square Publishing, LLC
243 5th Avenue, Suite 136, New York, NY 10016

Copyright © 2019 by Cavendish Square Publishing, LLC

First Edition

Library of Congress Cataloging-in-Publication Data

Names: Best, B. J., 1976- author.
Title: Length and width / Arthur Best.
Description: First edition. | New York : Cavendish Square, [2018] |
Series: Properties of matter | Audience: K to grade 3.
Identifiers: LCCN 2018012333 (print) | LCCN 2018013661 (ebook) |
ISBN 9781502642219 (ebook) | ISBN 9781502642202 (library bound) |
ISBN 9781502642189 (pbk.) | ISBN 9781502642196 (6 pack) |
Subjects: LCSH: Length measurement--Juvenile literature. |
Measurement--Juvenile literature. | Matter--Properties--Juvenile literature.
Classification: LCC QC102 (ebook) | LCC QC102 .B47 2018 (print) | DDC 530.8--dc23
LC record available at https://lccn.loc.gov/2018012333

Editorial Director: David McNamara
Copy Editor: Nathan Heidelberger
Associate Art Director: Alan Sliwinski
Designer: Megan Metté
Production Coordinator: Karol Szymczuk
Photo Research: J8 Media

The photographs in this book are used by permission and through the courtesy of: Cover Slawomir Gawryluk/Shutterstock,com; p. 5 Africa Studio/Shutterstock.com; p. 7 Flashpop/Stone/Getty Images; p. 9 Neil Fraser/Alamy Stock Photo; p. 11 Elena Pavlovich/Shutterstock.com; p. 13 Gorvik/iStock/Thinkstock.com; p. 15 Slobo/E+/Getty Images; p. 17 Sudpoth Sirirattanasakul/Shutterstock.com; p. 19 Home Studio/Shutterstock.com; p. 21 Dorling Kindersley/Getty Images.

Printed in the United States of America

Contents

Things are made of **matter**.

All things have length.

All things have width.

You can **measure** them.

4

5

You can find length.

You measure with a **ruler**.

You start at one end.

You go to the other.

Things can be long.

They have a lot of length.

Roads are long.

Poles are long.

9

Things can be short.

They don't have much length.

A paper clip is short.

An ant is short.

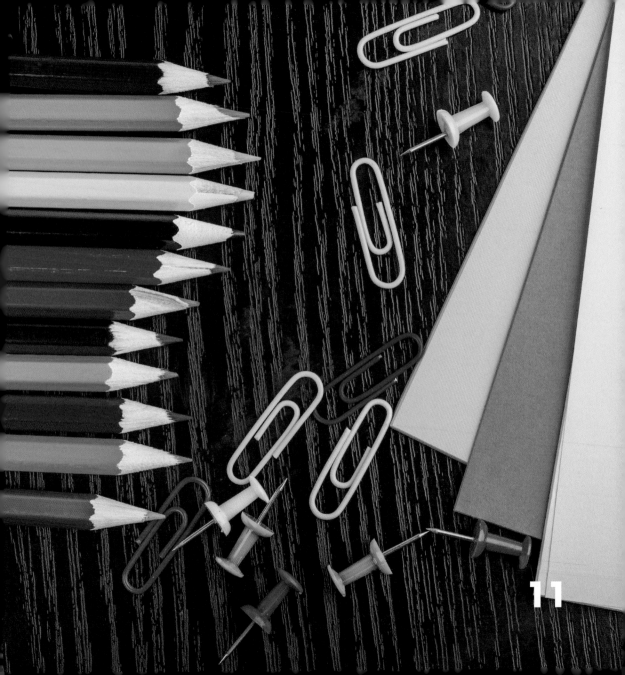

You can find width.

You start at one side.

You go to the other.

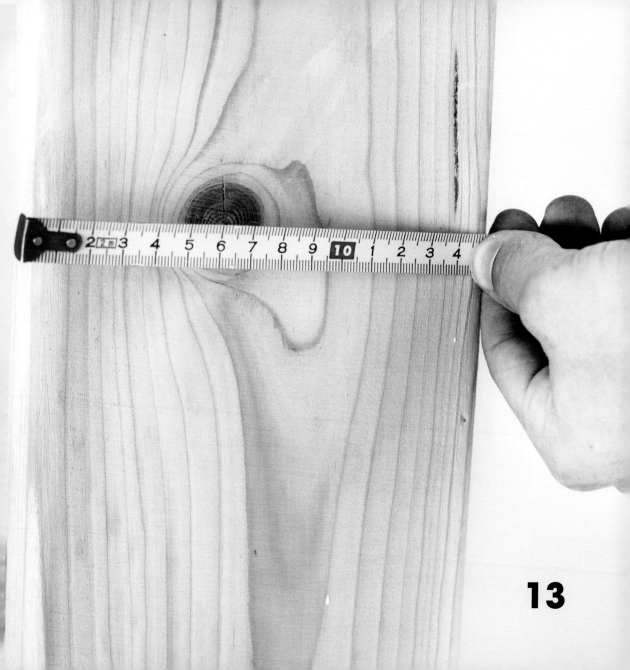

13

Things can be wide.

They have a lot of width.

A field is wide.

An oven is wide.

15

Things can be **thin**.

They don't have much width.

But they can be long!

A nail is thin.

A hair is thin.

16

17

Things can change length.

A new pencil is long.

Then it is used.

It gets shorter!

19

Length is always the longer side.

Width is the shorter side.

But **squares** are the same on all sides.

The length and width are the same!

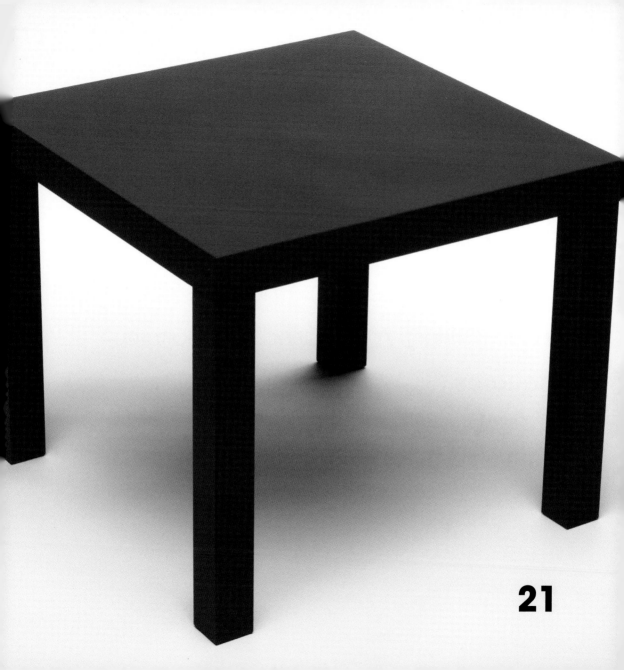

21

New Words

matter (MAT-er) What objects are made of.

measure (MEHZH-er) Find the size of.

ruler (RU-ler) A tool used to measure.

squares (SKWAIRS) Shapes that have four sides and the same length and width.

thin (THIN) Not wide.

Index

About the Author

Arthur Best lives in Wisconsin with his wife and son. He has written many other books for children. He has a length of five feet and nine inches.

About

Bookworms help independent readers gain reading confidence through high-frequency words, simple sentences, and strong picture/text support. Each book explores a concept that helps children relate what they read to the world they live in.